8 Practical Steps
to
Conscious Mothering

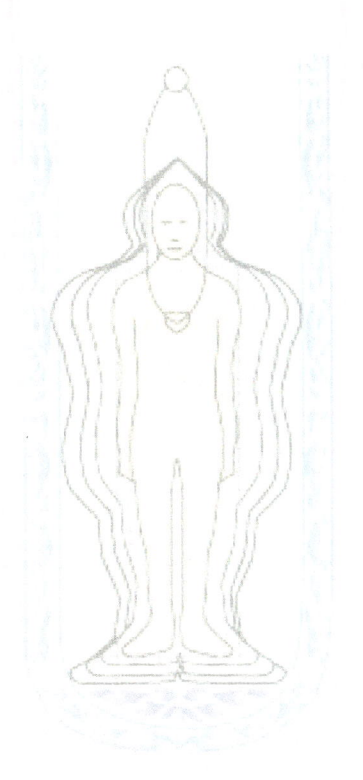

Annette Rugolo

with Foreword by Marie Diamond

8 Practical Steps to Conscious Mothering © 2013 by Annette Rugolo
All rights reserved

Preface

Many books, articles, and movies have been created over the years that focus on the importance of finding a mentor and being mentored. In your search for a mentor, it is essential to find one who can help you move through the overload of information and tools that are available. We all need a mentor who understands the need for fast transformation and real results in a time when people are feeling overwhelmed and confused by this overload of information.

I knew I found such a mentor when I met Marie Diamond. Her wisdom, knowledge, and tools have helped me find my way through all of the chaos and confusion that a fast-paced world can create.

My vision and goal is to become this kind of mentor for others, and by using the tools in this e-book, you will begin cutting through the density that exists around you in order to begin living with clarity and purpose the vision for your life and to support your children in living theirs.

Marie Diamond and I share a vision for an enlightened world. I am happy you have found your way to this information because I believe you play an integral part in this vision. We need conscious mothers raising conscious children to create a conscious world. Thank you for your willingness to step forward!

Remember, if you want to transform any aspect of your life, you need to change something about your life. Do not be afraid of change…it will set you free from whatever is limiting you at this moment. Take a step toward something you want in your life and trust that the universe will support you.

These 8 steps are just the beginning. When you are ready for more, we are here, ready to assist. Check out our websites at *www.consciousguideformothers.com* and *www.mariediamond.com*.

Wishing you a Transformed Life!
Annette

Foreword

We are in an age of rapid change and at a time when everything seems to be speeding up. Because change is necessary if we are going to create the kind of world we all wish for, then we need to learn how to best move with the changes. I knew at a very young age that I wanted to be part of this global change and provide ways to assist others with this change.

Through change, we are able to build something new and, as in the building of anything new, it is important to have the right tools available. I have dedicated my life to bringing forward some powerful methods that have been used by millions of people around the world, and I have witnessed so many wonderful changes in people's lives when using them. I am happy to see many of them presented by Annette Rugolo in this e-book.

I know that when you apply these practical steps in your life, you will begin to see some positive changes within days. My methods create change in both your environment and in yourself, but the most important change is within.

As a mother of 3, I have personally used my own methods to help my children reach their full potential. When people meet my children, they know instantly that there is something unique and different about each of them. The confidence and self-assuredness of each of my children comes through, and their light shines wherever they go.

I met Annette Rugolo in 2002 when she became a student of the Inner Diamond method. It has been a pleasure to witness her transformation over the past years as she continued to study and implement the Inner Diamond meditations, Diamond Dowsing, and Diamond Feng Shui into her life. Her commitment to uplift herself and others catapulted her to the position of Vice President of my company, a position she held from 2007-2012.

I encourage you to listen to what she has to say in this e-book because her wisdom and heart have guided many over the years. I have been witness to her challenges and successes since she began, and I celebrate her profound commitment to transforming herself and others. Her knowledge comes from her years as a mother, grandmother, step-mother, and foster mother. She has transformed and uplifted the lives of her own family. When you begin using these practical steps, you will be transformed and uplifted, too. This is a necessary e-book for our times.

Wishing you an Enlightened Life,
Marie Diamond*

* To read more about Marie, see the More About Marie Diamond section at the end of the book.

Introduction

My own path to becoming a conscious mother has been one filled with victory and loss, clarity and confusion, moments of great sorrow and times of celebration.

The road to consciousness is not a smooth path; it is filled with trial and error. My purpose for writing this e-book is to help moms everywhere experience less of the trial and error and more of the victory, clarity, and celebration.

There is more to becoming and staying a conscious mother than what is written here, but these 8 practical steps will help you begin or will help you re-focus. They will give you the opportunity to create transformation quickly for you and your family.

Within this e-book, you will have access to some amazing tools. I have personally used these tools for my own transformation and have witnessed magic happen in my life, in my family, and in the lives of my clients.

The tools promoted throughout this book were created and introduced by Marie Diamond, a transformational leader, speaker, and author. They are profound tools of transformation and, like tools of any kind, you need to learn how to use them and apply them to your life.

Each of the steps will help you look at a certain aspect of life and will give you some easy tools to incorporate. The steps are not listed in order of importance, though, so take a look at each step to see which one resonates with you the most. That will be the place you will want to begin.

For more information and ways to help you and your child, visit my website at *www.consciousguideformothers.com*.

To find out more about Marie Diamond and the programs she has created, visit *www.mariediamond.com*.

Connect with Color, Transform with Intention, Live in Light,
Annette

Tubes of Light Meditation

Before we begin discussing the "Eight Practical Steps to Conscious Mothering" for transforming your life and supporting your children, we will start with a foundational step that will help you connect with the quantum field. This step is an essential meditation called the 'Tubes of Light'.

Beginning each day with the Tubes of Light meditation will help you create a strong connection to the quantum field and you will be able to navigate through the steps in this book with greater ease. You will see with more clarity which will allow you to focus on those areas that are most in need of transformation. You will call into your daily experience the help and support you need and you will begin to trust that this support is available to you throughout your day.

The meditation/visualization I am introducing to you here is the cornerstone of all of the work you will be doing as you move through this material. It is a defining tool that enhances and supports everything else you do each day.

With this meditation, you will become empowered to call into your life and your daily experience certain colors of quantum frequencies that will help you feel more balanced and calm. In this calm, relaxed state, you will then be able to connect to a field of expanded possibilities and solutions. You will begin operating from an elevated level of awareness and you will start seeing your life through a clearer lens.

Download the 15-minute meditation at:

http://consciousguideformothers.com/8steps/.

The Steps

1. De-Clutter Your Space   3
2. Create Beauty   9
3. Activate Personal Best Directions 13
4. Add Color to Your Life   17
5. Replenish Yourself   23
6. Create Boundaries   31
7. Protect Yourself and Your Children 39
8. Create a Vision Board   43

1. De-clutter Your Space

Having a de-cluttered home is one of the first and most important steps to conscious mothering. Why? Because clutter stops the flow of energy—or chi—in the home. Energy needs to move, and if there is no place for it to move because of obstructions, it becomes stuck and stagnant. This eventually affects the people living in the home, and their lives can become stuck in the same patterns, the same chaos.

Scientists have discovered that we have something called neuro-mirrors in our brains. Neuro-mirrors are tiny, microscopic mirrors that reflect everything back to us in our environment, and it creates a picture for us of how the world looks. If your child is growing up in a cluttered home, their picture of the world becomes a picture of clutter.

Clutter not only takes up space in your home, it also takes up space in your head. People living in cluttered spaces tend to be more stressed and anxious. If you see piles of stuff everywhere you look, it tends to send your brain into overload when there is only so much your brain can handle. If you clear out and organize your environment, you can then make space in your head to handle more. A cluttered space can also affect your sleep and your dreams.

When my step-daughter, Chelsey, moved to San Diego at the same time my husband and I did, she lived with us for a few months until she could find a place of her own. Like most busy young adults, her room tended to be cluttered more often than not. After about a week, she started having bad dreams that did not stop, even after making sure she was not sleeping in any negative energy.

Two months after we moved in, my friend, Marie Diamond (a

Feng Shui Master), came for a visit and Chelsey graciously gave up her room. Marie shared with us the next morning that she was having some terrible dreams in that room and asked if the negative energy had been cleared. We said it was and when she took a closer look at the room, she realized that a corner of the room was severely cluttered and was stopping the flow of spiritual energy into the room for both her and Chelsey. She spent some time explaining to Chelsey the importance of de-cluttering a room and gave her some basic feng shui tips. Chelsey, not wanting any more bad dreams, did as Marie suggested and the bad dreams ended immediately. She was also able attract better work situations and made friends more easily. In fact, she was able to move to her own apartment within a month.

I have always been an organizer and a "de-clutterer." Maybe it's because of all of the moves I have made over my lifetime. At some point, I started choosing wisely what items I wanted to keep moving around. Maybe it's an innate gift, but I love to organize spaces. I especially love the feeling after a space is organized and seeing the reaction of that organized space on other people. People seem to breathe a sigh of relief as they feel lighter and more serene. Many are becoming very aware of the effect clutter has on their lives, and for those who do not de-clutter easily, there is a growing profession of organizers ready to meet this need.

Before I give you some tips on how to de-clutter your space, I first want to share with you some of the negative effects (besides those listed above) that clutter can have on your life:

- Extra income spent on storage units to fit all of the stuff that doesn't fit into your house. (More that 10% of all Americans now rent additional storage space.)
- Accidents created by cluttered stairways, hallways, basements, and garages.
- Loss of time spent looking for lost or misplaced items.

- Wear and tear on vehicles when there is no place to park in the garage.
- Health hazards created by unknown vermin living among the clutter.
- Late fees incurred on bills when statements are misplaced or lost.

Many times, clutter is less about collecting stuff, and more about not being able to let it go. If you have trouble letting go of your stuff, consider what underlying causes there might be, and then start visualizing what your life might be like without it.

The underlying cause for one person I worked with whom needed to remove clutter from outside of her office didn't believe that she had the time to clear it out. When she focused on how it would feel to have it gone, the universe created the time and help she needed.

An additional underlying cause can also be the energy in your home. If there is just one area or room in your home that seems to attract clutter, there is most likely some energetic disturbance in that area that is resistant to space clearing. If you continually enter a room with the intention of de-cluttering only to become tired, anxious, or angry within 10 minutes of being in the room, you are reacting to an energetic disturbance in your home. In this case, your home needs to be dowsed and cleared of the disturbance. For more information on dowsing, please visit my website at *www.consciousguideformothers. com* and click on the Conscious Homes tab.

Some tips for de-cluttering your space:

- If you feel overwhelmed by all of the clutter, start small. Start with a cabinet, a corner of a room, or your desk. Sometimes, just having one small space de-cluttered will motivate you to want more.

- When de-cluttering, make four separate piles:
    a. one with item to throw away or recycle (garbage)
    b. one to give away to Goodwill or the Salvation Army or to some one you know who may want the item
    c. one with items to put into storage
    d. one with things you wish to keep
- If you have a hard time parting with something, put it into storage and see if you miss it after a few days or weeks. Chances are, you will forget all about it. If that's the case, take it out of storage and give it away.
- My rule of thumb for clothes: If I haven't worn a piece of clothing for over a year, I get it out of my closet. Do you have one of those pieces of clothes that you paid good money for but, every time you put it on, you take it off again? It's time to give it away to someone else who will wear it.
- While you're trying to de-clutter, do not purchase a new item without removing something it's going to replace.
- Do not take on other people's belongings. If you are storing items for family members or grown children who have moved into their own place, ask them either to take their belongings or to get rid of them. Make them responsible for their own stuff.

Remember, if you feel overwhelmed, start small but keep going. It's also good to ask someone for support who is good at organizing spaces. You don't have to do it alone, and it can be a lot more fun doing it with a friend.

Start visualizing your home already de-cluttered. Ask the universe for help and be open to receiving it when it shows up.

By de-cluttering your space, you will create an environment where the energy can flow. Your home will feel lighter and so will you.

I've included the following images to help you begin feeling and visualizing the difference between a cluttered and de-cluttered space.

2. *Create Beauty*

Creating Heaven on Earth ... it is a saying that I became aware of years ago and have come to understand at a deeper level over the years. It has many meanings and implications but one of them has to do with beauty. When you envision heaven, whatever your idea of heaven means to you, what do you picture? Do you picture a place of disorder, ugliness, and darkness or do you picture a place of light, color, and beauty? If you are like most people, your picture will be the latter of the two.

As a conscious mother, it is important—even crucial—that you learn how to create heaven on earth in your own home. If we are going to do this for the world, we need to focus on our homes first.

Start by paying attention to how you feel when you enter people's homes and how you feel when you enter your own home. Do you feel like bolting the minute you walk in the door or does the home invite you to sit and enjoy the space for a while? Do you hold your breath until you can get out the door or do you find yourself exhaling and relaxing into the space?

Creating beauty is the next step after de-cluttering. If you create space in your home, what do you fill it with?

I was fortunate to grow up in a family where my mom knew how to create space and beauty in our home. So, naturally, as a young wife and mother, I intuitively wanted this for my family. We didn't always have the money to buy expensive items so I learned how to create beauty with a few simple, inexpensive items.

Inexpensive framed artwork is a good way to start. Make sure the images are ones that reflect what you want your child to see in his or her world. Images of war and death (even abstract allusions) are not images to impress on your child's young psyche. Family photos in beautiful picture frames are always a great addition. Other examples include pictures of nature, images that create a serene environment or uplifting images of hope and love.

- Pillows, area rugs, and throws are a great way to add color to a room. Look at color combinations that are appealing and help you feel uplifted.

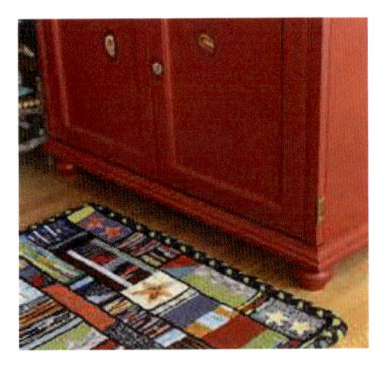

- Plants and flowers have been my mainstay throughout the years because they bring both color and life to the home. If you feel you don't have a green thumb, choose an easy-to-care-for plant (philodendron's are great), purchase a beautiful silk arrangement, or keep your home filled with fresh cut flowers.

When purchasing your plants, choose plants with soft, round

leaves that create a gentle feel and appearance. Cacti and plants with spiked, knife-like leaves are not the best choices for creating an inviting feel for a home.

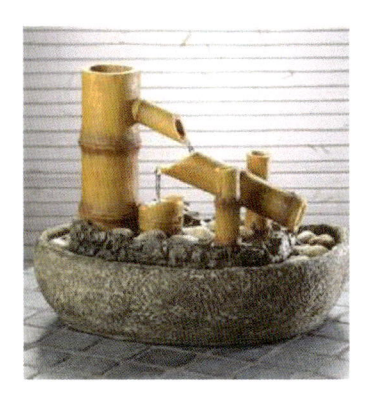

- A water fountain is another way of adding more beauty and the flow of chi to a home. Visit your local garden store or department store for fountains that will fit your space. Bubbling fountains are great but make sure the noise isn't too intrusive.

If this task seems overwhelming at first, again, just like de-cluttering, take small steps. Start with one room of your house or a corner of a room, and create space and beauty there first. Many times, a few small steps will help you become more energized and excited about moving forward.

3. Activate Personal Best Directions

The ancient art and science of feng shui has been used for thousands of years around the planet and has recently been introduced to the West. There are two schools of thought regarding feng shui: black hat feng shui and the traditional or compass feng shui. Marie Diamond, the feng shui master featured in the movie The Secret and whose information is presented here, is a master of the Traditional Chinese school of Feng Shui. She has created her own method called Diamond Feng Shui.

A unique aspect of traditional feng shui is the use of your personal directions based on the day you were born. There are nine directions in all but the ones we will be focusing on here are your four best directions. When you activate these directions in your home or office, you align yourself with the energy of the universe that supports you.

Your four best directions will support you in four areas of your life: Career, Relationships, Health, and Wisdom. Once you know what your four best directions are, you can "activate" them with images and colors that will connect you and your home to the universal energies that support these areas in your life.

A seven-year-old girl I recently worked with was having difficulties in her relationships, and she kept attracting friends that either manipulated or bullied her. I helped her mom find her daughter's four best directions (you will find a link to help you find yours at the end of this section) and told her how to activate her daughter's relationship corner of her bedroom with specific colors and to add pictures of her daughter with friends. The only pictures that were in her bedroom before this time were pictures of her standing alone. The message she was sending the universe was that she was alone and, as a result, her experiences supported that.

After making these changes in her relationship corner of her bedroom, her relationships at school began to change. Now other girls ask her to be her friend.

She was also having trouble going to sleep at night and would usually cry herself to sleep. After her mother moved her bed so that her head was pointing toward one of her good directions, she now goes to bed without incident and is asleep within five minutes.

A very simple way to support you and your family is to find out everyone's four best directions and to activate these directions in your home. You will activate your child's directions only in their bedroom, and will activate your directions for the rest of the house because you are the owner. You can increase the effectiveness of these activations by activating your office and bedroom, as well.

A few simple tips to help you get started:

- When you sleep, your head points toward one of your best directions.
- Face one of your best directions while awake.
- Have children sit facing their wisdom direction when doing homework or studying for a test to increase their effectiveness.
- Support their success at school or in activities by placing trophies, awards, newspaper articles, and pictures in their success direction.
- Activate their wisdom direction with pictures of mentors or teachers they admire.
- Activate their health direction with images depicting wholesome activities and anything that supports their health.
- Make sure everyone is feeling supported and included at family meals and meetings by having everyone face one of their four directions.

- When you activate the directions with images, be aware that you are sending a message to the universe 24/7, so make sure the images match what you want.

- Discovering and activating your family's best directions is a great activity to do with your child, and most children I know really get excited about doing this. Unless they are too young and still non-verbal, include them on these activations. If they are too young to understand the concept, lay out some choices for them and let them choose for themselves what they want.

When you are ready to get started, go to *http://consciousguideformothers.com/8steps/* to find out the four best directions for everyone in your family.

Marie Diamond, as a feng shui master, has created the method of enhancing feng shui by including the 24 quantum colors of the universe.

Once you have activated the directions with images, you can then add a second activation of color. Each of your four best directions has a specific color, or frequency, that will also send a strong signal to the universe. For instance, the color to activate your success is royal blue, health is green, relationship is rose, and wisdom is yellow. When combining images and color, you will not only strengthen your activations, you will also create beauty in your home.

To activate your four best directions with color, find images, items, or cloth with the color and place them in the direction you are activating. For instance, if you would like to activate your or your child's success direction, find a royal blue item or image to place in that direction. When you do that, you are "activating" it and connecting it with the quantum frequency of success. It connects your field of success beyond the 3rd dimensional experience to a quantum leap in the 5th dimensional experience, which will create a quantum leap in your or your child's area of success.

When I first learned this information, I understood it as a way to create a billboard to the universe. I took a look at everything I had on the walls of my home and asked myself if they were the messages I wanted to send to the universe every second of every day. If they weren't, then I changed the picture or other object. I was amazed at how quickly making these changes altered my experience.

Activating your four best directions is one of the easiest ways to begin transforming your and your family's law of attraction. It is an effective and fun way to spend some time with your child in helping them create the life they want.

Marie Diamond has created the Diamond Feng Shui home study course for those wanting to learn more about feng shui. To learn more about Diamond Feng Shui, visit *http://www.mariediamond.com*.

4. Add Color to Your Life

Before I was introduced to the Quantum Colors of the Inner Diamond, the only colors you would have seen when opening my closet were black, white, and red. Pretty monotone and very boring!

When attending my first Inner Diamond Meditation seminar created by Marie Diamond, I was introduced to the 24 quantum colors. The 24 quantum colors are frequencies that exist all around us, but until we become aware of them, we don't always know they are there. These colors are like those we see in a rainbow. Even though the colors of the rainbow are always there, we only see them under certain atmospheric conditions.

After being introduced to these colors, I transformed my wardrobe by adding green, blue, peach, pink, and others into my clothes choices. And when my wardrobe changed, so did my life. Once I understood that every color has a certain vibration or quality, I started using color to add a specific quality in my life that I felt was lacking. For example, I felt at one time I took life much too seriously and I wanted to add more joy and fun into my life. Peach is the color for joy so I started wearing a lot of peach. I also purchased peach-colored candles and burned them a few times a week.

After about two weeks, I started noticing that I was attracting joyful, funny people into my life. I started seeing the humor in everyday events and I felt more joyful within myself. It was definitely a lighter feeling and I liked it.

Recently, when I walked into a well-known department store, I was amused to see what they had created at the entrance. Over the entrance was a canopy of colors with a sign that read, "Color Changes Everything." Looking at the shelves close to the entrance, the items were bright, colorful, and festive. I felt uplifted walking into the store, and I couldn't help but appreciate the person who came up with a great way to greet their customers!

When you begin adding color to your life through the clothes you wear and how you decorate your home, you are bringing vibrant, highly supportive energy around you.

Have you ever noticed how, as children, we wear colorful clothes and then, the older we get, we wear darker colors? This is just one indication of the loss of our inner child. When you give yourself permission to wear color again, you reconnect with the lightness in you that became dormant.

When I teach mothers about using color with their children, I recommend that they ask their young child what color they want to wear instead of what outfit they want to wear. One mother of a three year old did just that, and she was mildly surprised when her daughter chose fuchsia every day for the first week of school. After the second day of wearing fuchsia, she was pleased to see her daughter playing with the other kids instead of standing alone in a corner of the play yard when she picked her up from daycare.

When she found out that the color fuchsia stands for collaboration, it made sense that her daughter would choose it.

Like the child in the story above, we sometimes sub-consciously choose a color we need to help us in some area of our life. When people need to connect with their inner power, they may choose to wear the color blue. If they wear aqua, they may be looking for clarity. If they are in need of some tenderness, they choose pink. (Learning this, I have found it very interesting that more men are adding pink to their wardrobe.)

The 24 quantum colors, or frequencies, are available to you simply by knowing they exist. Each color represents an enlightened quality, and when you know the quality each color represents, you can begin choosing what you need for that day or week by wearing that color and activating the quality in your energy field and in your daily experience.

Another child, Mya, a 6-year-old girl, was having trouble falling asleep. When her parents were ready to paint her bedroom, they asked what color she would like her walls to be painted. She chose a combination of magenta (peace and harmony) and fuchsia (collaboration), and now she loves her room and falls asleep easily each night.

As adults we can reconnect with these colors, but it is important to understand that many children are innately connected with them. When you ask your young children about the colors they see around people, you may be surprised to know that they are still seeing their world in beautiful Technicolor vision.

My daughter and I were talking about this one day, and I was curious to know if her three-year-old daughter was seeing color. Later in the day, we went for a walk with my granddaughter. We casually started asking her questions about color. What color is your daddy? She immediately responded "green." And what color is your mommy? She responded "silver." Silver isn't a typical color that a three-year-old child is familiar with, so it really caught our attention and confirmed that she was seeing these colors around her parents.

The colors she saw around her mom and dad definitely fit what was happening in their lives at the moment. Her dad was doing some inner healing work at the time and her mom was reconnecting with something inside of herself that had been lacking. When we reconnect with one of the aspects of these colors, we remember who we are and have always been.

When working with children, I always ask them what their favorite color is. One nine-year-old girl living in a home with negative energy that I was there to dowse responded "black." If your child is drawing with or wearing nothing but black, there is something that is preventing them from seeing these quantum colors. It might be the negative energy of the home, their bedroom, or something attached to their energy field that is preventing them from seeing the full spectrum of light and color.

One young woman came in for a personal consultation wearing black clothes, and black eyeliner, fingernail polish, and lipstick. Her hair was dyed pitch black and her entire energy field was devoid of light. The last time I had seen her was two years before and, at that time, she was bright and full of light. Something had happened in the two years since I had last seen her.

I quickly found out the family moved to a new house eighteen months earlier. As I asked some questions, I also discovered that, after the move, she started hanging out with a different group of friends—a group that carried a negative attitude toward life. Further, her grades had deteriorated and she just wasn't very happy.

When checking the energy of her bedroom, I found that she had been sleeping next to a negative energy field and she had taken on the darkness of the negative energy. We dowsed and cured the negative energy, cleared her energy field, and, when I saw her two months later, she had transformed. Her hair was her natural auburn color, she was wearing light colors, and her energy field was again bright and full of light. More importantly, her life had changed as she returned to her studies and attracted a more positive group of friends.

Color is a natural state of being for us. If we are devoid of color, either within us or in our environments, our lives will reflect it in so many ways. It becomes difficult for us to feel passionate about something, or our lives may feel chaotic or hopeless. We might experience low-level anxiety, frustration, or anger. Something is missing, but we don't know what.

If you are ready to bring color back into your life, there are two ways to begin:

1. Download the color chart of the 24 Quantum Colors and qualities, and begin using them in your home, for yourself and for your children. [Visit *http://consciousguideformothers.com/8steps/*

2. Purchase the Inner Diamond program to connect with the 24 Quantum Colors in a powerful way and to learn how to use these frequencies of light to transform your life and to support your home and your family. [To purchase, visit *https://mariediamond.infusionsoft.com/go/idb/arugolo/*.]

When you start bringing in the quantum colors around you, they will begin to awaken something within you, and you will soon find out that "Color Changes Everything."

5. *Replenish Yourself*

If you are one of those moms who feels as if everything and everyone comes before you and you are the last to receive what you need, this chapter is for you!

I was that kind of mom for a few years during my late 30's and early 40's. At the time, we had chosen to take on four teenage Vietnamese foster children and, along with my two teenage daughters, we created a recipe ripe for burnout. My day started at 6am and ended at midnight, going non-stop with a full-time job, grocery shopping, cooking, and cleaning, along with teaching a confirmation class, participating in a church music choir, and volunteering for a myriad of other duties at our church.

After about 12 months of a non-stop schedule, I found myself crying every morning on my way to work. I was exhausted but I didn't know what to do. I started drinking more coffee to have the energy to get through the day, and I ignored signals of exhaustion and illness to just keep going. I felt powerless to change my daily routine and I couldn't see a way out of where I was. After two years of this, I experienced constant sinus infections, allergies, and an onset of adult asthma. People who had met me a few years before kept asking if I was okay. I heard my voice respond that everything was just fine, but I was screaming inside.

Things eventually calmed down a bit as new homes were found for two of the foster children and I started saying no to more requests from our church. By this time, I was so depleted physically, mentally, and emotionally, it would take me two years to return to balance.

I am writing this chapter with hopes that I can prevent just one mother from having the experience I had.

Since recovering, I have met many women who have had or are having a similar experience. Looking from the outside in, I can now see how easy it is to spiral out of balance and to become a person who completely ignores the signs and signals the body is giving us.

The first step in changing this destructive pattern is simply to take some time each day to replenish. I can hear it already … but I don't HAVE any time left in my day for myself! And to that I say, yes you do. You have the time, just like everyone else, but you have to become aware of it and give it priority.

I can tell you right now that if you don't start taking some time for yourself, someone else will be taking care of you in a few years. As a mom who wants to continue to be there for your family, it is absolutely crucial that you begin doing this.

The analogy I like to use when helping moms take time for self is the message we hear on airplanes before take-off: "In case of emergency, place the oxygen mask on yourself first before placing it on your child." Many moms have forgotten that in order to be there in the long run for their family, they first need oxygen for themselves.

How do you take the first step? First learn how to say "NO." This was a big step for me and I still remember the feelings of guilt that swept over me the first time I told someone "no." I felt like I was letting everyone down. But then I saw that they just moved on and found someone else to volunteer for the task, and I realized after a while that it was no big deal to them if I said yes or no. But it was a big deal for me!

You may even have to say "no" to your children and your husband. More guilt ensues until you realize again that they are just fine without you being there every moment of the day.

Even if I had taken time for myself in the midst of my crisis, I'm not sure I would have known what to do with it. I certainly did not know how to replenish myself and I'm not sure I even knew what that meant at the time. If you are having the same difficulty, here are a few suggestions:

- Take a warm bath with a Do Not Disturb sign on the door

- Find a well-lit, comfortable place to read a favorite book

- Spend some time in nature—visit a botanical gardens

- Take a walk or ride a bike

- …really, do any exercise

- Buy yourself a bouquet of your favorite flowers

- Treat yourself to a manicure or pedicure … or both

- Schedule a massage or reflexology appointment

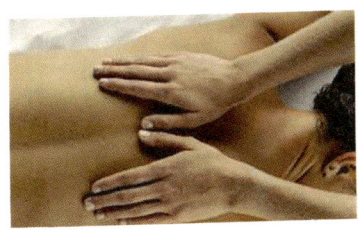

- Meet a friend for tea

- Get your child involved if needed

- Breathe!

When you're ready to make a bigger commitment to yourself, sign up for a yoga or exercise class or an art or dance class. Start with one hour a week and build up from there.

The ultimate way to replenish is by taking 15 minutes a day for the Tubes of Light meditation. When adding this meditation/visualization to your day, you will tap in to a source of energy in the universe that is available to you 24/7.

Created by Marie Diamond, the Tubes of Light meditation is used by hundreds of thousands of people around the world. When incorporating it into your life on a daily basis, you will begin to connect with your inner strength and to feel more supported by others, and you begin releasing whatever patterns of limitations you might have that are stopping you from seeing expanded possibilities and solutions for your life.

When I began incorporating this meditation into my life, I felt I had found an inner wellspring of energy and sustenance that I had not known existed until that moment. I have personally witnessed thousands of students and clients transform their lives simply by adding this 15-minute meditation to their day. If you had any trouble with the other steps in this book, then try this meditation before you re-try the step—you may find it easier afterward.

If you are ready to tap into a source of unlimited potential, visit *http://consciousguideformothers.com/8steps/* to download your free audio of the Tubes of Light meditation.

As I look back on those crisis years, one thing I realize is that I was constantly waiting for someone to give me permission for me to take care of myself. I eventually learned that I was the only person who could give that permission, which I needed in order to do whatever it took for my own health, sanity, and well-being.

By listening to your inner voice and intuition and by taking the steps you need to be healthy and whole, you will not only change your life but everyone's around you, too. You will also be setting a great example for your children as they watch you transform from stressed and overwhelmed to happy and balanced.

As you take your first steps, know that I am here tomhelp you with any step along the way!

6. Create Boundaries

As a conscious mother, it is important to create safe boundaries for your children. And even though they may squawk and holler about them, at some level, they are also appreciative.

In a world filled with an abundance of toys, electronics, computer games and TV, sweets, snacks, and fast food, it is crucial we guide our children to find a balance among all that is available to them.

Setting boundaries for some children can actually change their personalities. The parents of a seven year old were frustrated every morning when she could not stay focused on doing what needed to be done to leave the house on time. They came up with a solution of writing out her morning schedule and posting it on the wall. She is allotted a certain amount of time to dress herself, eat breakfast, brush her teeth, and comb her hair. She now has a schedule that she loves to follow and is usually ready before it's time to leave the house.

Creating boundaries for your child can take on many forms, but I will be focusing here on what I consider to be the top three: Sleep, Diet, and Technology.

Sleep

One of the first ways to create boundaries is to look at the bedtime situation. This is not just a good idea for your children, but for you, too. We need sleep to replenish and nourish our bodies as well as integrate what we have experienced during the day. Without the proper amount of sleep, we are not able to function at our full potential during the day.

   Along with making sure you and your children are getting enough sleep (check out the Table of Requirements), curing the negative energy in your environment is one of the first things you can do to assure your family is getting the sleep they need.

   Dowsing for a family of a 3 year old, I discovered she was not sleeping in her bed and would crawl in her sister's bed every night after everyone was asleep. When checking the energy she was sleeping in, I found two geopathic stress lines crossing her bed. Negative vibrations are the result of geopathic stress lines caused by underground water or fault lines and of EMF energy from power lines, radio towers, or cell phone towers. These occurrences affect a person's ability to experience a sound, healing, and replenishing sleep. Once you live in a dowsed home, you will very likely experience a profound difference in your sleep pattern and typically will wake up feeling energized for your day.

How Much Sleep Do You Really Need?	
Age	Sleep Needs
Newborns (0-2 months)	12-18 hours
Infants (3 to 11 months)	14 to 15 hours
Toddlers (1-3 years)	12 to 14 hours
Preschoolers (3-5 years)	11 to 13 hours
School-age children (5-10 years)	10 to 11 hours
Teens (10-17)	8.5-9.25 hours
Adults	7-9 hours

Source: National Sleep Foundation

Symptoms that are most often shared with me when I dowse a home include a reluctance to go to bed, a habit of getting out of bed and moving to another bed or sofa in the middle of the night, tossing and turning all night, snoring, anxiety, irritability, and more. The importance of an energetically quiet and calm room is a primary focus when supporting sound sleep for you and your family.

Diet

Setting boundaries around food and diet are crucial. With all of the sweets, fast food, soft drinks, and snack foods so readily available, our kids need us to create healthy boundaries around their food intake. Poor food choices lead to our bodies and minds breaking down, and make us more susceptible to fatigue, illness, and emotional and mental imbalances.

Information is readily available on the effects of diet on our kids, and I have focused on this aspect on my website at length. With new ways to test the effects of chemicals, preservatives, and artificial ingredients in our food, we are finding that many children are highly sensitive to and are negatively affected by many of the foods they regularly consume.

The first step is to reduce the amount of fast foods, sweets, snacks, and soft drinks in your child's diet. The challenge is not only to reduce foods that are not nutritious but to replace these items with whole, healthy foods.

Studies have been done over the past 15 years regarding the effect of food on a child's learning capacity. Children starting the day with a healthy breakfast do better in school, overall, than children who don't.

Lunch programs have been a focus for many studies over the years, and schools that changed their lunch programs to include healthier food options consistently showed improved test scores and grades for the children involved in the studies.

Many parents are becoming aware of the effects of sugar on their children and are limiting the amount of soda their child consumes. Most 12 oz. cans of soda contain up to 9 teaspoons of sugar! The alternative sugar-free sodas contain artificial sweeteners that have their own set of side effects.

I realize it is difficult to set boundaries around your child's eating habits, especially when you are not with them all day, every day. When setting a good example at home, it will be easier for your child to make better choices when they are not at home. When possible, send healthy snacks with them to encourage them to choose those over vending machine snacks or other unhealthy items.

I've listed some things below that have worked for me and my family and have added a few known resources, as well. For more tips, visit my website at *www.consciousguideformothers.com*.

- **Start slow.** Making drastic and sudden changes usually don't work. The mothers I have worked with start by replacing one unhealthy snack with a healthy one per week.

- **Involve your children.** By involving your children, you will not only be helping them make better choices when they are not at home, but you will be showing that they are a valuable part of the process.

- **Try to find a time when you can share a family meal.** Many families eat on the run or constantly eat fast foods because of a hectic work, school, and activity schedule. Find one or two times a week that will work in everyone's schedule, involve the children in the preparing of a meal, and enjoy a good, home-cooked family meal.

- **Never bribe your child with food.** Using food as a reward or punishment creates an emotional connection with food that will create problems in the future for both you and your child.

- **Learn about your food.** Educate yourself about the chemicals, pesticides, and other substances used in our foods that could be having adverse effects on you and your children.

For more information on the effects of food and to find healthy alternatives, visit my website at *www.consciousguideformothers.com*. You will find some great resources to help you create healthy, great tasting meals and snacks for your family even if you don't have a lot of time. You will also find solutions for your child with food sensitivities.

Technology

The third major area where boundaries are needed is around the use of technology. Technology is great, but like anything else, we need to use it in a balanced way. If your child's entertainment is centered around the TV, computer, iPods, etc., it is important to provide balance for them.

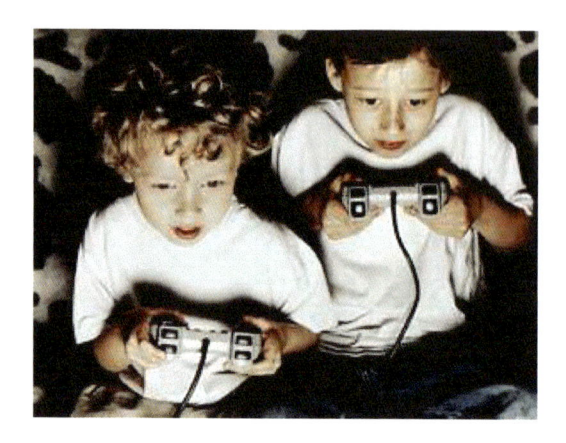

Scheduling activities in nature will create balance not only for your children but for you as well.

Sunshine is important because it provides us with natural Vitamin D. Try to be in the sun for about 20 minutes a day. Either early in the day or late afternoon is best. If you live in an area with little or no sunshine, make sure you supplement your diet with Vitamin D.

Nature not only provides a great source of Vitamin D but it also helps our bodies energetically cleanse. With our abundance of technology comes the abundance of exposure to EMFs ... Electro Magnetic Frequencies. Although there are contradicting reports about the risks of EMFs in our environments, my own experience has shown that children have an increased sensitivity to the EMFs around them. Although the effects may not show up on tests, I have seen people transform when the EMF energy in their environment is reduced or cured through the technique of dowsing. (See the Conscious Homes page at *www.consciousguideformothers.com*.)Time in nature helps our bodies release the EMF's, or electrosmog, built up in our systems from too much exposure to technology. Walking barefoot in the grass is the best way for this energy to be released. Earth absorbs and recycles this energy and you feel refreshed and balanced again.

I have spent time with 3- and 4-year-old children who intuitively know this. When playing outside with my 3-year-old granddaughter, she insists we run around in the grass with our shoes and socks off. After about 15 minutes, she is done and ready to move on to the next game.

If you are not able to be outside to release the EMF's or electrosmog from your energy fields, there are products created to help.

One such product is the quantum energy ring, which is designed to transform the energy in your energy field and to release anything that it has collected or attracted throughout your day or week. It also helps people who are sensitive to EMF energy.

I am someone who is very sensitive to the EMFs emitted from computers. When I first began using a computer regularly for my business, I could only sit at it for 30 minutes at a time before becoming tired and fatigued. When I found out about the quantum energy ring, I placed one of the large rings on the floor between me and my computer and was thrilled when I could sit there for more than 30 minutes at a time!

The quantum energy rings not only help with reducing EMFs in your energy field, they also uplift the energy of a person or a room wherever they are placed. People find that sitting in one while praying or meditating, studying, working, and even sleeping helps them feel more focused and clear. Many people place one under their car seats to help them stay more alert while driving.

I have created a free e-book that lists the many uses for the Quantum Energy Rings and you can download it by visiting *http://www.consciousguideformothers.com/8steps/*

Along with time in nature, providing your child with ways to express creativity through art, games, music, dance, etc., will activate their creative mind and will help them in the future to find creative solutions in their life. These activities don't always need to be organized or scheduled activities that are added to your "to do" schedule, but try to make them spontaneous. Dancing with your child in the living room to their favorite song can be all that your child needs sometimes to re-connect outside the world of TV and computer games.

If you are looking for some creative activities for you and your child, I found this great website that will help you get started: *http://www.creativekidsathome.com/activities.shtml*.

As a conscious parent, do not be afraid to set and create boundaries for your child. It is easier to create healthy boundaries when you understand the long-term benefits for your child. I encourage you to continue to find out more about the effects of diet, sleep, and technology for you and your children.

7. Protect Yourself and Your Children

We protect our property and cars with home and car insurance, our access to medical care with health insurance, and spam on our computers with a firewall. We protect these things in our life much more than we protect our own energy fields.

Everything in our universe is energy including the energy we create with thoughts and emotions. Not all of what we and others create is good, light, and uplifting energy. We create things like worry, fear, jealousy, judgment, hatred, and so on. Once these energies are created, they float around in our atmosphere.

Did you ever meet someone you couldn't wait to get away from? Someone who was spouting hatred and judgment of everything and everyone around them? At that moment, you were feeling their energy and you instinctively knew that it wasn't a good thing to continue to hang around them.

When we walk around with unprotected energy fields, we can easily take on or absorb any of the energy that is floating around us, created by others. This energy can then influence how we think and feel, and it can even affect the way we make decisions. It is difficult to stay above these negative vibrations if they are strong enough. They have a subtle influence on us without us being conscious of it.

To demonstrate, let's look at how this works on a larger scale.

Back in the 1970s, a company created a doll and named it the Cabbage Patch Doll. The doll became so popular that, for some reason, it created a craze and every young girl absolutely had to have it. Because of this craze, absolute pandemonium broke out as parents fought over these dolls in department stores and went to great lengths to have one for their own daughter.

When there is enough energy created by enough people, this energy takes on a life of its own and, even if you or your daughter had no desire to have this doll, you might have become swept up in the momentum that it created.

We can see similar experiences when kids start hurting each other over a special kind of jacket that everyone has to have or when an entire country goes into fear because of terrorist threats.

These are big examples to demonstrate my point, but there are also other energies around us that can wear us down on a daily basis. Anyone who is around other people at any point in their day become exposed to picking up the energy created by others.

A necessary step to becoming a conscious mother is to understand the importance of protecting you and your children from other people's energy. When you protect yourself, you begin to be aware of the energy created by you and the energy created by others.

Why is this important? If you want to transform your life, you first need to know when you are responding to your own emotional and mental patterns and when you are being influenced by someone else's emotional and mental patterns. Is the fear you are feeling yours or is it an energy created by an entire group of people who are simultaneously reacting to an event?

This is one of the first steps in mastering your life and it is a very important one.

As a conscious mom, you will not only have the opportunity to protect yourself energetically, but you will be able to protect your child as well. If your child is under the age of 14, you can visualize and do a protection meditation for them. Once they reach 14, you will need to ask their permission to do this for them. Why? At 14, the personality locks in and permission is required to enter their energy field. You can also teach them the Tubes of Light meditation that they can do themselves.

Tubes of Light diagram

The mother of a six-year-old learned the meditation and, one day, while she was doing the meditation her son came in the room and asked what she was doing. She told him she was protecting herself and he immediately wanted to learn how to do it, too.

After that, he asked his mom every day to help "put on his lights." After about a week, he told his mom that his cousin needed the lights, too, and can they do the lights for him? His mom, of course, said yes and one of their daily practices before school was to "put their lights on."

Another young boy, who was four years old at the time, had a hard time sleeping and needed the lights in his bedroom on all night. He was afraid of something in his room and couldn't tell his mom what it was. He consistently had dark circles under his eyes from lack of sleep.

His mom learned the Tubes of Light meditation and immediately taught it to her son. The first morning after doing the meditation together, her son woke up after a solid night's sleep. At breakfast, he shared with his mom a dream he had during the night. He and his friends were on a boat. The boat capsized and they all ended up in the water. But he assured his mom that it was okay because he had his life jacket on and he saved all of his friends. It was a great confirmation for his mom that the Tubes of Light meditation worked.

When people ask how they will know if this meditation will work for them or not, I simply tell them to try it for a week and see if they see or feel a difference because of it. Do it for you and your child, and then pay attention to changes.

You already have access to the Tubes of Light meditation in Chapter 5. It is a download you can use for yourself. I have created a second version that will take you through the meditation for yourself and then help you energetically connect with your child or children to protect them, too.

To download the Mother/Child Tubes of Light, visit *http://consciousguideformothers.com/8steps/*

Remember: You are able to do the protection meditation for your children up until the age of 14. Once they turn 14, they will either need to do the meditation themselves or you will need to ask their permission to continue to do it for them. The best practice is to teach your child the meditation, explain the importance of it, and have them take the responsibility of doing it themselves.

8. Create a Vision Board

Your life now is the outcome of everything you have felt, thought, and visualized up to this moment in time. If you want to transform any aspect of your life, it is crucial you change something to create a different outcome. I know that change can be difficult. We all have a tendency to settle or to settle in. There is a familiarity or comfort level in our lives that is sometimes hard to break through.

Incorporating all of the steps presented here will help you begin creating a different future. The final step is to begin visualizing the future you do want. When you hold a vision for your future, it is necessary to hold it in focus for a long period of time. If it is too difficult to keep your focus on your future, then it is also difficult to overcome all of the negative messages and images you have created, bought into, or allowed in the past. The more you can hold a thought, idea, or image of your future in your awareness, the faster it will happen. If you are not strong enough to hold that new vision in place then worry, fear, and doubt tends to trickle in and muddy the clear picture you started out with.

Luckily, there is a simple solution for creating and holding the vision want to happen: Create a Vision Board.

When you create a Vision Board, you are focusing on what you desire for your success, relationships, health, and spirituality. Using your four best directions that you accessed in Chapter 3, you will use these directions on your vision board and create a message that you would like your vision board to hold for you, without fear, worry, or doubt.

Once you finish your Vision Board, you will place it in your success direction of your bedroom or office to activate more intensely your success direction. The universe now sees your message 24/7 and you simply allow the law of attraction to work for you.

A word of caution: when creating your Vision Board, make sure your images and messages are something that is attainable for the coming months or year. Some people, when first starting out, place messages on their boards that are not attainable and then think their Vision Board is not working for them.

For example, if you are having financial difficulties, are out of a job, and have limited education at this point in time, it is fairly reasonable to assume you will not be making a salary of $500,000 this next year. It is something that might be attainable in the future, but not without taking steps that may manifest that kind of salary.

When creating your Vision Board, it is important that you stretch yourself and expand your vision for your life beyond what it is now, but be practical in asking the universe to manifest too far beyond your current circumstances.

Once you create your Vision Board, check it from time to time to see what has manifested for you. Once something has manifested, thank the universe, and replace it with an image that will stretch you again. Remember, your Vision Board is not a static image to the universe. It will constantly change and grow as you transform your life.

Vision Boards are a fun activity to do with your child and, as you help them create a vision for their life, you will help them stretch and expand and they will begin seeing bigger possibilities for their life.

Some things to keep in mind as you begin:

- Bring your Vision Board to life with beautiful images, color, words, and phrases that create the picture you want to send to the universe. Images from magazines or printed from the internet are a great place to start. Include photos of family, friends and co-workers. Cut out words or phrases from magazines or make your own with colored markers or with your computer.

- Make it your own and help your child make it their own. Don't influence them with what you want for their life, but allow them the time to express what they really want for their life. You might be surprised at what comes out.

- Add to your Vision Board experience by creating a Family Vision Board with a vision of what your family wants for the world.

- Fine tune your Vision Board by creating one just for your success, one for your relationships, one that focuses on your health, and one for your wisdom. These can then be placed in your four best directions.

Vision Boards are a great way to explore and to expand possibilities for yourself, and they are a great way to spend time getting to know your child's dreams for their life.

To download a sample Vision Board Map, visit *http://consciousguideformothers.com/8steps/*

Marie Diamond has created an audio program that will teach you more about creating your Vision Board and how to use them to create a life aligned with your purpose. To purchase this program, visit *https://mariediamond.infusionsoft.com/app/manageCart/showManageOrder.*

Conclusion

I hope you have found these 8 Practical Steps to Conscious Mothering helpful. Like any changes that are made in life, start slowly and incorporate the steps and the tools at a pace that is comfortable for you. Some will find they are ready to dive in while others will want to "test the waters." Whichever pace is good for you, trust it. When using and incorporating the Tubes of Light, you will find your own rhythm and will move through this material at your own speed.

Many times, people want to see huge, instantaneous changes in their life. Although this can happen, most of the changes are going to be subtle and it is our job to stay awake and become aware of even the subtle changes. Small changes made over time will lead to big transformations.

The changes I remember noticing were usually things that disappeared from my daily life ... things like feelings of discomfort or fatigue, or a feeling of not being present or connected with my life or people around me. Those were good things to have gone. Sometimes it's those persistent feelings of inadequacy or not being good enough that disappear. What disappears is then replaced with something transformational ... feelings of confidence, hope, and joy are just some of what will come back to you. Life begins to feel more vibrant and alive.

I once was in a place in my life that I didn't like very much. What I have come to know and understand about these places in our lives, is that they are gifts. These are the times we begin searching for something beyond our current circumstances. We begin asking for help, looking for solutions, and expanding our horizons beyond what we currently know. When we take advantage of these times, they will lead us to greater heights and depths than we thought existed.

Thank you for joining the ranks of conscious moms, committed to raising conscious children and creating the enlightened world we all wish to have.

Connect with Color, Transform with Intention, Live in Light

Your Guide,
Annette Rugolo

annette@annetterugolo.com
www.consciousguideformothers.com

More About Marie Diamond

Marie Diamond is a globally renowned Transformational leader—featured in the worldwide phenomenon "The Secret" and seven other motivational documentaries (The newest is The Gratitude Experiment, April 2013), who uses her extraordinary knowledge of quantum physics, the Law of Attraction, and Feng Shui energy to help people transform their environments and their lives.

Her clients include A-list celebrities in film and music (like Steven Spielberg, Rolling Stones), top selling writers (Rhonda Byrne, Jack Canfield), leaders from Fortune 500 companies (Amoco-BP, Exxon, and Total Fina), governments, and royal families. Marie Diamond combines her intuitive gifts, the growing science of energy flow, ancient wisdom, and modern tools to enlighten homes, businesses, and people. She is known for her passion to help create Enlightened leaders around the world.

She is a Founding member of the Transformational Leadership Council, created by Jack Canfield, and President of the Association of Transformational Leaders in Europe (www.ATLeurope.eu).

She has students and clients in more than 185 countries. You can connect with her for executive coaching, consultations, seminars, online courses, e-books, and home study courses at www.mariediamond.com and energy products at www.mariediamonddowsing.com. You can also train with her for certifications as a Feng Shui and Dowsing Consultant.

She lives in the South of France with her husband and her 2 youngest children.

She is a bestselling author and her books have been translated in more than 10 languages.

Facebook: http;//www.facebook.com/mariediamond8888

A more detailed biography can be found on Marie at: http://www.mariediamond.com/index.php/meet.

For more information:

Connect with Marie Diamond at Office@mariediamond.com

Marie Diamond Global Ltd.

272 Kensington High Street, Suite 89 in W8 6ND

London, United Kingdom.

More About Annette Rugolo

Annette Rugolo is an international speaker, teacher, and consultant with clients and students in North America, Europe, Australia, and Asia.

Annette started teaching transformational seminars in 1999 and began her teaching career with the Marie Diamond Network in 2002, teaching both the Inner Diamond Meditation and Diamond Dowsing Methods. She is currently a Master Instructor for Marie Diamond Global and has personally trained students in over 20 countries.

In 2007, Marie Diamond, the global transformational leader featured in the popular movie "The Secret," hired her as the Vice President of her company—a position Annette held until 2012. Annette's business relationship with Marie Diamond Global has continued as she is currently the North American Coordinator for the Diamond Dowsing Teachers and is licensed to operate the Marie Diamond Dowsing website.

Together with her husband, Tony, she established Life Abundant Resources in 2005 for the purpose of manufacturing the dowsing tools and quantum energy rings for Diamond Dowsing.

Recently, Annette started her own company, Conscious Life Resources, to bring conscious resources through new channels. Using her experience as a mom of 40 years, a foster mother, step-mother, and grandmother, she created Conscious Guide for Mothers in order to spiritually assist mothers and children.

Prior to 1999, Annette's experience in the business community included almost 20 years of holding management positions in the hotel and insurance industries.

After a personal transformational crisis in her life in 1995, she became a licensed massage therapist (Cayce/Reilly School of Massage in Virginia Beach, VA) and had several massage businesses in North Dakota.

Other major complimentary health areas she became certified in were yoga, Cranial Sacral Therapy, and Qigong, teaching yoga for several years along with other transformational workshops.

Her desire to learn how to transform her own life and to share this knowledge with others ultimately attracted her to the Inner Diamond Meditation methods. With Marie Diamond as her mentor, she studied the transformation methods taught in this program since 2002 and has mastered many aspects of these universal transformational principles.

As Annette's quest for knowledge expands, Conscious Life Resources and her work with Marie Diamond Global continues to bring this knowledge to the world.

Made in the USA
Charleston, SC
30 May 2013